A WALK INTO ETERNITY

An Inevitable Expedition of the Human Race

Gbenga Mathew Owotoki

A WALK INTO ETERNITY

Copyright © 2014 by Gbenga Mathew Owotoki

ISBN 978-978-937-516-5

PUBLISHED BY Hephzibah Network Publishing

ALL RIGHTS RESERVED TO THE AUTHOR...

All scriptural quotations are from the King James Version (KJV) of the Bible, unless when stated otherwise.

A WALK INTO ETERNITY

Table of Contents

Dedication 5

Acknowledgment 6

Preface 7

THE JOURNEY BEGINS 9

    WHO DOES GOD CALL YOU? 9

    WHAT WILL BE YOUR LEGACY? 11

    DOES GOD REALLY CARE? 13

    TIME ILLUSION 18

THE PROVISION 20

    ULTIMATE SACRIFICE 20

    THE PRAYER LINE 26

    THE SOURCE WITH AN ENDLESS RESOURCE 28

    "WHY ME LORD?" 35

    FREEZING THE ENEMY'S JAW 37

    A RARE TREASURE 39

SOUL PREPARATION 44

    THOUGH IT GLITTERS… 44

    THOU ART INEXCUSABLE 46

    SOLD OUT.. 49

    GOING DEEPER... 51

    EVIL COMMUNICATION CORRUPTS… 53

A WALK INTO ETERNITY

    FIREWORKS ARE TEMPORAL 55

    CLEAN UP YOUR MESS 57

    BUILDING YOUR HOUSE 59

CONTENDING FOR THE FAITH 62

    THE LETHAL BLEND 62

    GOD'S UNWAVERING STANDARDS 67

    WHY ARE YOU NOT HERE? 69

    WHERE IS GOD'S GLORY? 71

    BURNING AND SHINNING LIGHT 76

    CHANGING SHADES 80

    THE TRUE REFERENCE POINT 82

ETERNITY IS NON-NEGOTIABLE 84

    HOLD ON TO YOUR CROWN 84

    TIMELESSNESS 86

    DON'T IGNORE THE WARNINGS 89

    ARE YOU READY? 92

This is Important 95

Contact Details: 97

Other Books By The Author 98

Dedication

To my Lord and Savior Jesus Christ. You are the reason why I live; you are the reason why I breathe. Thank you for making this possible.

To My Jewel of Inestimable Value, my best friend and dearly beloved wife, Eunice 'Rock Owotoki, Thanks for your support, encouragement and prayers. You are the very best. Love you very much.

To my very own 'Pappi,' you have brought fullness to my life, love you loads, son.

Acknowledgment

A big God bless to all the leaders, officers and members of Hephzibah Network International Ministries for all the support over the years.

A special thanks to everyone that have played one role or the other in my journey so far. I appreciate you and say God bless you richly

Preface

Every man born into this world is on a journey into timelessness. Your life on this earth will determine which part of eternity you will end up. We are all in a race but many are running on the wrong track which leads into perdition and like the scriptures say, "Enter through the narrow gate. The gate is wide and the road is wide that leads to hell, and many people enter through that gate. But the gate is small and the road is narrow that leads to true life. Only a few people find that road" -Mathew 7:13-14 (NCV).

The world is heading for a plunge and more and more people are less mindful of where they will spend eternity. But whether we like it or not, everyone will certainly give an account of their life on earth. The things done in secret will be made open and light shone on activities carried out in the dark. Great surprises will greet many as they stand before the Great white throne judgment to answer for their time on earth. My question is: Are You Prepared? Are you

A WALK INTO ETERNITY

ready to face God's judgment? This is the time for you to take stock and consider your walk with Him. No jury will be able to bail you out if you are found wanting. Eternity is a certainty; it is non-negotiable. Your birth was only the beginning. You are a 'never dying soul.' Death is the door into timelessness. You will be standing alone; all your praise singers will not be there; they will be busy giving accounts of their lives too. Nobody will be there to defend you. The record books will be opened and there will be no room for denial. Are you prepared? Think about this!

For most of you, we may not get the chance to see face to face but I pray we all make it through those pearly gates and be welcomed into the warm embrace of our Savior. I pray the Lord will minister to your heart through this book and you will be better prepared for eternity.

CHAPTER ONE

THE JOURNEY BEGINS

WHO DOES GOD CALL YOU?

The issue is not about how you and I feel about what we believe or don't believe; it's about how God feels. It's not about how you and I call it; it's about how God calls it. The question is who does God call you? People may call you by different names and appellations, but what will stick eternally is the name that God calls you. Have you got a lot of praise singers around you, who sing your praise until your head gets bloated and keeps you feeling as though you're on top of the world? As wonderful as such feelings are, if God sees it differently, then you are merely living in the land of illusion. God has the final decision because He knows all things.

A WALK INTO ETERNITY

A major league baseball player hit the ball far out in left field. The bases were loaded. The one who was on 2nd base made it all the way to home plate, and he collided with the catcher. Immediately, one team yelled, "He's safe! He's safe! He's safe!" The other team yelled, "He's out! He's out! He's out!" Upon looking at both teams, the umpire calmly announced, "He is nothing until I call him."

What you perceive as accolades from men may draw condemnation from the Lord because He sees and tries the reins of your heart. You may be reading this today and feel like you deserve commendation for things you have done, but instead you have been the object of a smear campaign. Not to worry, man may condemn you, but when God commends you, you are settled. Beloved, once again I ask you, who does God call you? Seek to please Him and not man, and He will call you by your name on that glorious day when the roll is called up yonder. Will you be there?

A WALK INTO ETERNITY

WHAT WILL BE YOUR LEGACY?

Your legacy is summed up in what you have done with your life. You may have built a great legacy here on earth but what does God think of you at the end of the day? There is nothing wrong with building a great legacy. We have great people whose legacies still speak for them after they are long gone. We also have villains in history who have also left behind a bad legacy. There was a study conducted by New York state sociologists on two families: the Max Jukes family and the family of Jonathan Edwards. The head of the Max Jukes family (not his real name), was an unbeliever, a man with no obvious sense of morals, and he married a girl with similar values. Among the known descendants of the Jukes family, over 1200 of them were studied. Of those, 280 were professional vagrants, 130 were sent to a penitentiary for an average of 13 years each. 7 of them were murderers, 100 were alcoholics, and 128 were prostitutes. Of the 20 who learned a trade, 10 learned it in a state prison.

A WALK INTO ETERNITY

None of them made a significant contribution to society. On the contrary, they cost the state of New York $1,308,000. What about the Jonathan Edwards family? He came from a Christian family and married a girl with similar values. Among his descendants, 100 became clergy men, missionaries, or theological professors. Over 100 became college professors. Over 100 became lawyers (30 of them judges). Over 60 became physicians, and over 60 became authors. There were 75 army/navy officers, and 13 presidents of universities. There were numerous giants of industry, several members of congress, 3 senators, and one became vice president of the United States. What type of legacy are you going to leave behind? It's such a simple thing to believe in and serve God and teach your children to do the same. This is a gift that requires no money, yet is invaluable. It is a gift that will last through out eternity.

A WALK INTO ETERNITY

DOES GOD REALLY CARE?

Does God really care? You have probably asked yourself this question at a point in your life journey. Maybe you have had bouts of disappointments. Maybe you have offered prayers that have gone unanswered. Regardless of whatever might have happened, always know that God really cares and certainly listens. He is never too late and He's always been there. I read a story of Ruby Hamilton, a businesswoman in her fifties, who was stunned at the loss of her husband of 32 years in a car accident. Her anger and disappointment went deeper than the more typical expression of grief, though. She had become a follower of Christ in her late twenties, but her husband didn't share her new found interest in spiritual things. Nonetheless, she had set about praying for him feverishly and unceasingly that he would come to know the Lord. And one day when she was praying, she felt a wave of peace wash over her, and that still small voice assuring her that her husband would be okay. She eagerly awaited the day when her husband would surrender his life to Jesus. And now this! What do you do when faith doesn't make sense? When God doesn't seem to be answering or opening doors or being found? Ruby Hamilton stopped living for God.

Roger Simmons was hitchhiking his way home. He would never forget the date – May 7th. His heavy suitcase was making him tired and he was anxious to take off his army uniform once and for all. Flashing his thumb to an oncoming car, he lost hope when he saw it was a black, sleek new Cadillac. To his surprise the car stopped.

The passenger door swung open. He ran toward the car, tossed his suitcase in the back, and thanked the handsome, well-dressed man as he slid into the front seat. "Going home for keeps?"

"Sure am."

"Well, you're in luck if you're going to Chicago."

"Not quite that far. Do you live in Chicago?"

"I have a business there," the driver said. "My name is Hamilton."

They chatted for a while, and then Roger, a Christian, felt a compulsion to share his faith with this fiftyish, obviously successful business man. But he kept putting it off, till he realized that he was now just 30 minutes from his home. It was now or never.

"Mr. Hamilton, I would like to talk to you about something very important." Then he simply told Mr. Hamilton about the plan of salvation, and ultimately asked him if he would like to receive Jesus as his Savior and Lord.

The Cadillac pulled over to the side of the road. Roger expected that he was about to get thrown out of the car. Instead, the businessman bowed his head and received Christ, then thanked Roger, saying "This is the greatest thing that has ever happened to me."

A WALK INTO ETERNITY

Five years went by. Roger married, had a couple of kids, and a business of his own. Packing his suitcase for a trip to Chicago, he found a small white business card that had been given to him by Hamilton five years previous. Once in Chicago, he looked up Hamilton Enterprises. The receptionist told him that it was impossible to see Mr. Hamilton, but he could see Mrs. Hamilton. A little confused, he was ushered into a beautiful office where he found himself facing a keen-eyed woman in her fifties. She extended her hand. "You knew my husband?"

Roger told her about how Hamilton had picked him up while he was hitchhiking home after the war.

"Can you tell me what day that was?"

"Sure it was May 7th, five years ago, the day I was discharged from the army."

"Anything special about that day?" she asked.

A WALK INTO ETERNITY

He hesitated, not knowing if he should mention how he shared the message of Jesus with her husband. "Mrs. Hamilton, I explained the gospel to your husband that day. He pulled over to the side of the road and wept against the steering wheel. He gave his life to Christ that day."

Explosive sobs suddenly shook her body. Finally getting a grip on herself, she sobbed, "I had prayed for my husband's salvation for years. I believed God would save him."

"Where is your husband, Ruby?"

"He's dead. He was in a car crash after he let you out of the car. He never got home. You see, I thought God had not kept his promise. I stopped living for God five years ago because I thought God had not kept his word!"

You see why I believe there will be a lot of surprises on that final day. Don't give up praying. Answers will definitely come. All prayers are answered. We fail to remember that "no" and "wait" are answers. But don't be in a hurry to give up on God. He truly cares for you and will make things to work out for the best of everyone involved.

TIME ILLUSION

There is this misconception people have about time; we think we've got plenty of time but in reality we are in a race against time because in this journey, there is not so much left. There is a fable which tells of three apprentice demons who were coming to this earth to finish their apprenticeship. They were talking to Satan, the chief of the devils, about their plans to tempt and to ruin men. The first said, "I will tell them that there is no God."

Satan said, "That will not delude many, for they know that there is a God."

The second said, "I will tell men that there is no hell."

Satan answered, "You will deceive no one that way. Men know even now that there is a hell for sin."

The third said, "I will tell men that there is no hurry."

"Go," said Satan, "and you will ruin men by the thousands."

The most dangerous of all delusions is that there is plenty of time. The time of the second coming of Christ is not known. Obtain your salvation today, now, and insure yourself against the ever-ticking clock.

CHAPTER TWO

THE PROVISION

ULTIMATE SACRIFICE

Jesus took our pain upon Himself. He suffered on the cross so we could enjoy freedom. He sacrificed His life to rescue us from eternal death. What will be our story as Christians if Jesus did not resurrected? Death could not hold Him captive, and even in the grave, our Jesus is Lord. Let your hope be built on Jesus; all other ground is sinking sand.

I read a story of two brothers who were playing on the sandbanks by the river. One ran after the other up a large mound of sand. Unfortunately, the mound was not solid, and their weight caused them to sink in quickly.

A WALK INTO ETERNITY

When the boys did not return home for dinner, the family and neighbors organized a search. They found the younger brother unconscious, with his head and shoulders sticking out above the sand. When they cleared the sand to his waist, he awakened.

The searchers asked, "Where is your brother?"

The child replied, "I'm standing on his shoulders"

With the sacrifice of his own life, the older brother lifted the younger to safety. The tangible and sacrificial love of the older brother literally served as a foundation for the younger brother's life.

Jesus has paid the price for you to live life to the fullest. There is so much available in JESUS, but unfortunately, we have only tapped so little from this Endless Reservoir. Let your heart pant after Him. Friends, when you seek Him with all your heart, you will find Him. He is waiting for you with His hands stretched out. The Scriptures says "If God is for you, who can be against you?" Certainly, no one! What a huge privilege we have in Jesus. Think about it!

There was an earthquake which wrecked havoc in one of the South eastern countries. When the rescuers reached the ruins of a young woman's house, they saw her dead body through the cracks in the walls. But her pose was somehow strange in that she knelt on her knees like a person who was worshiping. Her body was leaning forward, and her two hands were supporting an object. The collapsed house had crushed her back and her head.

With many difficulties, the leader of the rescue team put his hand through a narrow gap on the wall to reach the woman's body. He was hoping that this woman could still be alive. However, the cold and stiff qualities of the body told him that she had passed away. He and the rest of the team left this house and went to search the next collapsed building.

For some reason, the team leader was driven by a compelling force to go back to the ruined house of the

A WALK INTO ETERNITY

dead woman. Again, he knelt down and used his hand through the narrow cracks to search the little space under the dead body.

Suddenly, he screamed, "A child! There is a child!"

The whole team worked together, and, carefully, they removed the piles of ruined objects around the dead woman. There was a 3 month-old little boy wrapped in a flowery blanket under his mother's dead body. Obviously, the woman had made the ultimate sacrifice to save her son. When her house was falling, she used her body to make a cover to protect her son.

The medical doctor came quickly to exam the little boy. After he opened the blanket, he saw a cell phone inside. There was a text message on the screen that read: *"Dear baby, if you can live, always remember that I love you."*

Jesus paid the ultimate price for your redemption. Imagine Him taking up death that should naturally come to us and giving us LIFE in exchange. What a privilege to be called His child! I was once a candidate for hell but His blood cleansed me. And

A WALK INTO ETERNITY

like the woman who shielded her son, Jesus took upon Himself the judgment that was directly meant for us. Know this for sure that, if Jesus had not paid the price, there would have been no hope for the world. May His sacrifice not be in vain in our lives.

D.L. Moody once saw a man beat his dog at a zoo because he was mad at it. He had made a bet and boasted about the dog being so obedient, and when he tried to get the dog to do something, it wouldn't do it, and he lost his bet. He got so mad at that dog, and beat him continuously and mercilessly.

Finally, after the dog was wounded and bleeding and whimpering, he threw him in the lions' cage so that the lions would eat him. That poor whimpering, beaten, pitiful dog, was left standing, shaking on his bruised legs in the presence of that great lion. The lion came over to that dog and sniffed him. He began to lick the little dog. The dog laid down, and the lion laid down beside him, keeping him warm and licking his wounds. After seeing this, the man felt sorry for the dog, and told the person in charge of the lions' cage to let him have his dog back. The lion keeper, who had seen him beat the dog, said, "Fine, you can have your dog back. But you're going to have to go in there and get him yourself!"

That's the way it is with us. We were beaten, bruised, and battered by the devil and sin. Now the Lion of the Tribe of Judah, Jesus, has taken us in, healed our wounds, and now protects us from the enemy that once enslaved us! Nothing about our Lord Jesus Christ has changed through the centuries down to this very hour. His love has not changed. It hasn't cooled off, and it needs no increase. He has already loved us with an infinite love. It is the perfect love. The question is how much do you love Him? How much of your time do you devote to Him? Spending time with God is the key to our strength and success in all areas of life. Be sure that you never try to work God into your schedule, but always work your schedule around Him. The irony is that while God doesn't need us but still wants us, we desperately need God but don't really want Him most of the time. Think about it!

THE PRAYER LINE

Prayer is a very powerful tool for the believer. Jeremiah 33:3 says, "Call unto me and I will answer you and show you great and mighty things which you do not know." As we journey through this world, we cannot do without prayers. We need daily prayer shots to keep us in line and put us in the right shape as we gradually move into eternity. Tony Evans, a popular preacher from Texas, spoke of being on an elevator in a high-rise building. He said he'd never been particularly comfortable on such elevators. There was something about riding up and down in a little box several hundred feet off the ground that has never set well with him. He worried that something would go wrong.

A WALK INTO ETERNITY

One day it did. The car he was riding in got stuck in between two of the higher floors. He noted that some of the people in the car became frantic. They began to beat on the door hoping to get someone's attention. Others began to yell in hopes that their voices would get someone on the surrounding floors to come to their aid. But nobody heard their noise or their cries. Then Evans quietly made his way to the front of the car, opened a little door on the wall, and pulled out a telephone. Immediately, he was connected with someone on the outside. He didn't need to beat on the wall to get their attention. He didn't even need to speak loudly in the phone to receive their help. He could have whispered, and they would have heard him. In this world, we're going to get "stuck" in places where we aren't comfortable. Some people will beat against the walls, while others will cry out in dismay. But the person who trusts in the power of prayer knows there's Someone on the other end Who will hear their call and come to their aid. There is power in prayer. He has promised never to leave nor forsake you. Are you going through a very difficult time? All you have to do is dial the prayer line for direct access to Him. There is no network failure with this line. The reason why we don't get answers most of the time is because sin has clogged our transmitter. We must also be prepared for what the answer may be. It may not be what we want, but it will be what is best for us. God's hands are not shortened, and He is ever ready to save. Run to Him, and He will deliver you.

THE SOURCE WITH AN ENDLESS RESOURCE

How many times have we missed God's blessings because we can't see past our own desires? We dictate to God what He should do for us, and don't accept what His will is for our lives. You have been created for eternity, and some of what you are going through is part of the process meant to prepare you for this journey. He has a beautiful plan for your life. Let Him

A WALK INTO ETERNITY

take the driver seat, and although I am sure you will hit a few rocks, He will keep you safe through the bumps. He truly knows the bitter weary ways. Be patient, for He is bringing you to your desired final destination.

Dr. Bill Bright of Campus Crusade for Christ tells this story of a famous oil field called Yates Pool: During the depression, this field was a sheep ranch owned by a man named Yates. Mr. Yates wasn't able to make enough on his ranching operation to pay the principal and interest on the mortgage, so he was in danger of losing his ranch. With little money for clothes or food, his family (like many others) had to live on a government subsidy. Day after day, as he grazed his sheep over those rolling West Texas hills, he was no doubt greatly troubled about how he would pay his bills. Then a seismographic crew from an oil company came into the area and told him there might be oil on his land. They asked permission to drill a wildcat well. He gave his consent, and he signed a lease contract. At 1,115 feet, they struck a huge oil reserve. The first well came in at 80,000 barrels a day. Many subsequent wells were more than twice as large. In fact, 30 years after the discovery, a government test of one of the wells showed it still had the potential flow of 125,000 barrels of oil a day.

Can you imagine a millionaire living in poverty? The day he bought the land, he had received the rights to the oil and mineral on that land. Jesus is the Solid Rock; in Him is an endless reservoir of grace and provisions. The day you gave your heart to the Lord, you received the access code to explore the endless riches in Christ Jesus and when you stand on Christ, the Solid Rock, you invariably have access to all that is available through Him. When we follow Christ, we become joint heirs to the Kingdom of God along with Him. Mr. Yates lived on relief supplies even though he could hand out same to others in need. Unfortunately, many of us are under-utilizing God's resources that are at our disposal, but the truth is, how do you utilize the resources about which you are ignorant? There is so much we can become in and through God that we have not even realized. He has made all provision for you, and all you have to do is to discover the Source for the resources you seek. When you find the Source, the resource will never be exhausted. This is the secret of a life of abundance in Christ Jesus. There is an unlimited reserve in God but you have to 'dig' using God's Word as a tool to get there. In our story, the seismologists never discovered until they dug. How well do you know the scriptures? By this, I mean how well do you study the WORD? Are you more familiar with the news about 'world celebrities' than you are with God's Word? This is why your life is so shallow and you lack direction. When you are scripture saturated, the picture of eternity and where you are heading can never be hazy. I love this song written by Harry Loes:

A WALK INTO ETERNITY

> *"All that I want is in Jesus.*
>
> *He satisfies, joy He supplies;*
>
> *Life would be worthless without Him;*
>
> *All things in Jesus I find."*

Beloved all things are available and all things are possible through Christ who strengthens us. Jesus has made provision to make our walk less burdensome. Think about it! How can you fail with God? How can we miss it with Him navigating the 'boat' of our life? Now, don't get me wrong. Sometimes we may stagger but at the end of the day, His grand design is to bring us into His greater glory.

I read a story of a young man who was getting ready to graduate from college. For many months, he had admired a beautiful sports car in a dealer's showroom, and knowing his father could well afford it, he told him that was all he wanted. As graduation day approached, the young man looked for signs that his father had purchased the car. Finally, on the morning of his graduation, his father called him into his private study. His father told him how proud he was to have such a fine son, and told him how much he loved him. He handed his son a beautifully wrapped gift box. Curious, and somewhat disappointed, the young man opened the box and found a lovely, leather-bound book, with his name embossed in gold. Angry, he raised his voice to his father and said "With all your money, you give me a book?" and stormed out of the house. Many years passed, and the young man was very successful in business. He had a beautiful home and a wonderful family, but then he realized his father was getting very old, and thought perhaps he should go to him. He had not seen him since that graduation day. Before he could make arrangements, he received a telegram telling him his father had passed away, and willed all of his possessions to his son. He needed to come home immediately and take care of things. When he arrived at his father's house, sudden sadness

A WALK INTO ETERNITY

and regret filled his heart. He began to search through his father's important papers, and he saw the still gift-wrapped book, just as he had left it years ago. With tears, he opened the book and began to turn the pages. His father had carefully written him a loving note. As he read the words, a car key dropped from the back of the book. It had a tag with the dealer's name, the same dealer who'd had the sports car he had desired. On the tag was the date of his graduation, and the words "PAID IN FULL."

Yes, you have prayed, and you think what came back to you as an answer is not what you expected, but there is an answer in the unexpected. You must be patient. Read and study the scriptures. Great treasures are embedded therein. Many have missed great opportunities in life because they were in haste. Don't run ahead of God. Let Him lead the way. A man that is in haste is usually oblivious of his final destination. God's gift comes in several packages, and sometimes the package you get is not what you expect. Trust me, He knows what is best for this journey and His thoughts for you are thoughts of peace and not of evil. His grace is more than sufficient for you. You will make it to the end.

"WHY ME LORD?"

As we journey through life en-route to eternity, we are faced with many life challenges that will make us ask the question, 'why me Lord?' Tennis superstar, Arthur Ashe, died of AIDS, which he contracted from a blood transfusion during heart surgery. More than a great athlete, Ashe was a gentleman who inspired and encouraged many with his exemplary behavior on and off the court.

Ashe could have become embittered and self-pitying in the face of his disease, but he maintained a grateful attitude. He explained, "If I asked, 'Why me?' about my troubles, I would have to ask, 'Why me?' about my blessings. Why my winning Wimbledon? Why my marrying a beautiful, gifted woman and having a wonderful child?"

Ashe's attitude rebukes those of us who often grumble, "Why me, Lord? Why is God allowing this to happen?" Even if we're suffering greatly, we must not forget the mercies God pours into our lives. We are given such things as food, shelter, and friends and these are blessings that many are deprived of.

What about spiritual blessings? We can hold the very Word of God in our hands and read it. We have the knowledge of His saving grace, the comfort of His Spirit, and the joyful assurance of life everlasting with Jesus. As we remember the death and resurrection of our Lord and Savior Jesus Christ, let our question be: "Why Me, Lord? Why did He love me so much and die for me in particular on the cross?" Can you imagine what hope would have remained for believers if Jesus had died and not resurrected? But praise God, He broke the power of death, and the grave could not hold Him captive!

A WALK INTO ETERNITY

What an awesome feeling to be connected to Him through this great sacrifice on the cross!

Beloved, think about God's blessings and Jesus' death and resurrection, and ask, "Why me, Lord?" Then your grumbling will give way to praise. Let your praise ring out by worshiping Him with your life and showing how much you love Him for all He's done for you.

FREEZING THE ENEMY'S JAW

I read with great interest the synopsis of a research work about a small fish called the "Moses sole." It's a little fish that's found in the Red Sea. Back in the early 1970's, a group of researchers noticed something amazing about the little Moses sole. All the other fish in the same size and weight categories would be eaten by the sharks that are also found in those waters. But for some reason, these sharks would not eat the Moses sole. They found out that this

A WALK INTO ETERNITY

Moses sole has a very unique defense system. Anytime it senses some kind of danger, it naturally secretes poisonous toxins from its glands. These toxins literally cause the shark's jaw to freeze. There was a picture of a Moses sole inside a shark's mouth. The shark had obviously come in for the kill. All it had to do was bite down, and the Moses sole would breathe his last, but the shark couldn't do it because his jaw could not close due to the toxins released by the small fish.

What an interesting piece! It is not your size that matters, but He who dwells in you. You might be small, but He that is in you is greater than your enemy, the devil. As believers, we are meant to be poisonous to the devil and his cohorts. When the enemy comes with his diverse temptations and sin stirs you right in the face; don't flinch. Take your stand and do not yield to the intimidation of the devil. We should constantly emit 'toxins' that will freeze the activities of the devil around us.

A WALK INTO ETERNITY

A RARE TREASURE

A very wealthy man and his son loved to collect rare works of art. They had everything in their collection, from Picasso to Raphael. They would often sit together and admire the great works of art. When the Vietnam conflict broke out, the son went to war. He was very courageous and died in battle while rescuing another soldier. The father was notified, and he grieved deeply for his only son. About a month later, just before Christmas, there was a knock at the door. A young man stood at the door with a large package in his hands. He said, "Sir, you don't know me, but I am the soldier for whom your son gave his life. He saved many lives that day, and he was carrying me to safety when a bullet struck him in the heart. He died instantly. He often talked about you, and your love for art. "The young man held out his package."I know this isn't much. I'm not really a great artist, but I think your son would have wanted you to have this." The father opened the package. It was a portrait of his son, painted by the young man. He stared in awe at the way the soldier had captured the personality of his son in the painting. The father was so drawn to the eyes in the painting that his own eyes welled up with tears. He thanked the young man and offered to pay him for the picture. "Oh no sir, I could never repay what your son did for me. It's a gift."

The father hung the portrait over his mantle. Every time visitors came to his home, he took them to see the portrait of his son, before he showed them any of the other great works he had collected.

The father died a few months later. There was to be a great auction of his paintings. Many influential people gathered, excited over seeing the great paintings and having an opportunity to purchase one for their collection.

On the platform sat the painting of the son. The auctioneer pounded his gavel. "We will start the bidding with this picture of the son. Who will bid for this picture?" There was silence. Then a voice in the

A WALK INTO ETERNITY

back of the room shouted, "We want to see the famous paintings. Skip this one."

But the auctioneer persisted. "Will someone bid for this painting? Who will start the bidding? $100, $200?"

Another voice shouted angrily. "We didn't come to see this painting. We came to see the Van Goghs, the Rembrandts. Get on with the real bids!"

But still, the auctioneer continued. "The son! The son!! Who'll take the son?"

Finally, a voice came from the very back of the room. It was the longtime gardener of the man and his son. "I'll give $10 for the painting." Being a poor man, it was all he could afford.

"We have $10, who will bid $20?"

"Give it to him for $10. Let's see the masters."

"$10 is the bid, won't someone bid $20?"

The crowd was becoming angry. They didn't want the picture of the son. They wanted the more worthy investments for their collections. The auctioneer pounded the gavel. "Going once, twice, sold for $10!"

A WALK INTO ETERNITY

A man sitting on the second row shouted, "Now let's get on with the collection!"

The auctioneer laid down his gavel. "I'm sorry, the auction is over."

"What about the paintings?" the crowd shouted.

"I am sorry. When I was called to conduct this auction, I was told of a secret stipulation in the will. I was not allowed to reveal that stipulation until this time. Only the painting of the son would be auctioned. Whoever bought that painting would inherit the entire estate, including the other paintings. The man who took the son gets everything!"

What a great lesson embedded in this story. If you choose the SON then you have everything. So often we find ourselves distracted by the cares of life, and we fail to realize that, when we seek Him first, every other thing will follow and fall into place. There is always a catch in knowing Him. The gifts from the Lord are without regrets. You may have all that money can buy, but until you have Jesus you are far from having everything. There is a divine inheritance

A WALK INTO ETERNITY

connected to knowing the SON. Some people are just satisfied with their shallow knowledge of Jesus. The depth of what you know about Him will determine the height of your flight. Everything is available, but you need an 'access code' to claim these bounties. That access code can be found in Jesus. Decide today to climb out from the valley of complacency and walk into your inheritance. Take your walk with God deeper, and you will strike great treasures.

CHAPTER THREE

SOUL PREPARATION

THOUGH IT GLITTERS...

Not everything that glitters is gold. It may look attractive on the outside but it could be poisonous. The devil is a strategist, but our God is the Master of Strategies. The devil has been devising mischief and evil for a very long time, and he's got all kinds of experience with ways to 'shipwreck' any life. Countless generals of God have had their spiritual jugulars cut just by thinking they are invisible. "Let him that thinks he is standing take heed lest he falls." I read that the Eskimos of Canada and Greenland have an interesting, if rather cruel way of hunting bear. They will take a bone, preferably a wolf bone, and they will sharpen it at both ends. Then they will coil it through a process, freeze it in blubber and lay it across one of the paths the bears travel. As the bear comes along, he smells the blubber and in one gulp, he takes it and swallows it, not knowing that it's just blubber on the outside but on the inside there's this twisted, sharpened bone. And the minute he swallows it, he's dead. He doesn't drop down just yet, but every move he makes, every step he takes, causes that bone to twist, slash, and tear. Then internal bleeding starts and the Eskimos just follow the tracks of that bear until it dies.

Great men have fallen and some though recovered, their lives and ministries never remained the same again. Open your eyes, my friend! That thing may give you a temporal pleasure now, but buried in it is a 'sharp twisted bone' that can cause your spiritual walk with God to come to an unrecoverable halt. 'Can a man put fire in his bosom and not be burnt?' Just like the Eskimos in our story, the devil is lurking around, ready to strike when your guard is lowered. These days, you care less if you pray or even study the scriptures; little wonder why you are easily falling prey to the devil's scheme against your life. Beloved, no one is infallible. Your good speeches and oratory will not save you in the days of adversity. It is your depth in God that will keep you. Let's run from the shenanigans. Constantly look unto Jesus, the Author and Finisher of your faith. Keep yourself pure, for only the pure will see the Lord. Be prepared!

THOU ART INEXCUSABLE

What has happened to you? Yes I am talking to you! You used to love the Lord more than your very soul. The church had hoped for another Katherine Kuhlman during your fiery days. We had believed that there was yet hope for the church because we saw another Billy Graham in the making, but alas! The story is different today. The pendulum has shifted and the church is suffering because you drifted. His hands were twisted and his feet were useless. He can't bathe himself. He can't feed himself. He can't brush his teeth, comb his hair, or put on his underwear. Strips of fabric hooks and loops hold his shirts together. His speech drags like a worn out audio cassette. His name is Robert, and he had cerebral palsy. The disease kept him from driving a car, riding a bike, and going for a walk. But it didn't keep him from graduating from high school or attending a Christian University, from which he graduated with a degree in Latin. Having cerebral palsy didn't keep him from teaching at a junior college or from venturing overseas on five mission trips. He moved to Lisbon, alone, in 1972. There he rented a hotel room and began studying Portuguese. He found a restaurant owner who would feed him after the rush hour and a tutor who would instruct him in the language. Then he stationed himself daily in a park, where he distributed brochures about Christ. Within six years, he led seventy people to the Lord, one of whom became his wife. Robert could have asked for sympathy or pity, but he did just the opposite. On occasion, he would hold his bent hand up in the air and with smiles on his face declare, "I have everything I need."

The life of Robert is a rebuke to many of us. Many firebrands are now turning stone cold. Complacency in Zion has become a lifestyle, and the Church is in a state of comatose. If a man with this kind of debilitating sickness can be completely sold out to God, then we are inexcusable. Thou art inexcusable, oh man! We run up and down, everyone in the rat race leading to nowhere. It is what is done for Christ that will last. As good as achieving success in life is, when there is no record of your service to the Lord, it is but a wasted life. Let the testimony of Robert put us back on track. Look at your priorities, and serve the Lord while you can.

A WALK INTO ETERNITY

SOLD OUT

The church is presently undergoing a systemic persecution. The enemy has been unleashed and there is a vicious attack against the body of Christ. Whilst this is ongoing, the gospel of the Lord cannot be hindered, it must spread to every nook and cranny. It is time to be completely sold out. The matter of eternity requires haste. The day is far spent. We must all rise up and move and act as did the early Apostles. We must be consumed with the passion for evangelism as did the Moravian Brethren, who 200 years ago, formed one of the greatest missionary movements in history. Two of their members heard of a leper colony in Africa where no missionary was allowed to enter, but they feared that, once they returned home, the disease might spread through Germany. They volunteered to go into that leper colony for the remainder of their lives in order to present Christ there. How much has it cost us to serve Christ in terms of loss of money, comfort, reputation,

A WALK INTO ETERNITY

and health? If we are not willing to allow our Christianity to cost us everything that this world counts dear, we really do not know the meaning of serving God. The Lord is calling people today who will follow him in the pathway of the Cross, who are willing to be emptied of everything.

Vance Havner put it best when he wrote, "We need a heart warming... The early Christians did not need a shot in the arm every Sunday to keep them going. They knew Jesus, and they upset the world, worried the devil, gave wicked rulers insomnia, and started something the jails couldn't lock up, fire couldn't burn, water couldn't drown, and swords couldn't kill. You may be-little experiences and speak of the dangers of emotion, but we are suffering today from a species of Christianity as dry as dust, as cold as ice, as pale as a corpse, and as dead as King Tut. We are suffering, not from a lack of correct heads but of consumed hearts."

A WALK INTO ETERNITY

GOING DEEPER

When you are deeply rooted in God, the storms of life cannot uproot you. The enemy knows this truth, and that is why he will do everything possible to 'tie off your tap root' and by so doing, prevent your spiritual nourishment. Friends, I encourage you to go deep. Don't settle for the shallow end of the pool if you want to go far in life. You can take back your life from the devil and move forward to do great things for God!

The Japanese introduced a tree to the world that is called a Bonsai tree. It is measured in inches instead of feet like other trees. It is not allowed to reach anywhere near its full growth potential but instead grows in a stunted miniature form.

The reason for it growing in a stunted form is that, when it first stuck its head out of the ground as a sapling, the owner pulled it out of the soil, tied off its main tap root and some of its branch feeder roots, and then replanted it. Its grower deliberately stunted its growth by limiting the roots ability to spread out, grow deep, and take in enough of the soils nutrients for a normal growth.

What was done to the Bonsai tree by its owner is what Satan has purposed to do to the believer. He is going to try to tie off our tap root of prayer. He wants to limit what God supplies for our spiritual growth. If your spiritual roots are shallow, you cannot grow tall in God. The devil will do everything he can to cut off your roots and block your access to God's inexhaustible 'nutrients.' The glory of a tree is in the depth of its roots. Traveling the path to Heaven requires you to go deep – deep in the Scriptures, deep in communion with God, deep in holiness.

A WALK INTO ETERNITY

EVIL COMMUNICATION CORRUPTS...

"Be not deceived: evil communications corrupt good manners." – 1 Corinthians 15:33. Why will you allow someone to distract you from serving the Lord? Why would you be led astray as a result of the kind of company you keep? Many people have missed heaven because their friends led them astray. You don't have to miss it because someone close to you had deliberately made up their mind not to. Let us stay clear from everything that will defile us or whatsoever is abominable unto the Lord. I read a story about a lady called Jane. Jane knew she wasn't supposed to be at this party. But it wasn't her fault – not really. She was on her way to the movies, just like she told her parents, when she and Stephanie ran into a group of friends who invited them into the party. "Let's go!" Jane said to Stephanie. "I've always wanted to go to one of these parties." Jane was surprised at how easily the lie left her lips. At Jane's insistence, the two followed their friends to the abandoned warehouse. The party was already in full swing when they arrived. Later, when it became apparent that Jane was going to be late getting home, she found a pay phone and called her parents. "Mom? Stephanie and I decided to stop for pizza after the movie and ran into some friends. I'll be late, OK? Oh, yes, the movie was great. You need to see it. Yes, I'll see you soon, Bye." It was just a little white lie. What could it hurt? And what could it hurt to take her first drink of alcohol? She hated the taste, but the lie in her made her smile and say she loved it. And what could it hurt to dance with this great-looking guy? And what could it hurt to take another drink that he offered her? When Jane woke up the next morning, still groggy from the drug the 'cute' guy had slipped into her drink, she realized that her lies had hurt more than she could have ever imagined. Jane found out the hard way that lies are a set of stairs that go only one way: down. She lied to her friends. She lied to her parents. She lost the trust of her parents and her best friend, and she lost her innocence to a guy she never saw again.

A WALK INTO ETERNITY

Jesus explained that Satan is the father of lies. His tactics are so sly. If he can just get you to tell one little white lie today, then tomorrow he can take you one step further down the stairway with a bigger lie. Before you know it, you find yourself some place where you never intended to be, and Satan is laughing all the while. Don't hold Satan's hand and start down that stairway. Run to Jesus, hold His hand, and always speak the truth.

FIREWORKS ARE TEMPORAL

I have always relished every visit to the Disneyland in Florida and each time I have had the most exhilarating time visiting. The climax of the visit is a beautiful display of fireworks. I have never seen such display of fireworks like what I saw on those trips. There's something magical about those brilliant colors exploding against the dark sky.

A WALK INTO ETERNITY

But there's a problem with fireworks. They don't last. The same is true of many of the "firework" experiences in our lives. We fight and struggle for things that seem beautiful and alluring, but after we get them, their appeal disappears, just like fireworks. Maybe it's a shiny new car or speedboat. Maybe it's a big, impressive house. It might even be a promotion at work or a prestigious career.

So many of the things of this world are like fireworks. They promise happiness and fulfillment but can't deliver. TV commercials play on our emotions, making us believe that if we drive a certain kind of SUV or clean our floors with their super-efficient mop, we'll be happy at last. More often than not, all we feel is disillusioned.

If you've had enough of these "fireworks" experiences and the letdowns that follow, I challenge you to pursue the only thing in life that doesn't disappoint: a personal relationship with Jesus Christ. The astounding thing about loving God is that it actually gets better every day. Once you give your heart to Jesus, you'll have happiness and fulfillment that lasts into eternity and you'll never want to go back to those "fireworks" experiences again.

CLEAN UP YOUR MESS

God can make a message out of your mess. It is time for clean up. Paul the Apostle asked a very important question, "...Shall we continue in sin, that grace may abound?" (Romans 6:1). I cannot comprehend how people who deliberately live in sin would at same time lay claim to going to heaven. Satan will always look for means to continually hold us hostage to sin but you know you can be free.

Seven-year-old Tom decided one Saturday morning to fix his parents pancakes. He found a big bowl and spoon, pulled a chair to the counter, opened the cupboard, and pulled out the heavy flour canister,

A WALK INTO ETERNITY

spilling it on the floor. He scooped some of the flour into the bowl with his hands, mixed in a cup of milk, and added some sugar, leaving a floury trail on the floor which by now had a few tracks left by his kitten. Tom was covered with flour and getting frustrated. He wanted this to be something very good for Mom and Dad, but it was getting very bad. He didn't know what to do next, whether to put it all into the oven or on the stove (and he didn't know how the stove worked)! Suddenly he saw his kitten licking from the bowl of mix and reached to push her away, knocking the egg carton to the floor. Frantically, he tried to clean up this monumental mess but slipped on the eggs, getting his pajamas white and sticky. And then he saw Dad standing at the door. Big crocodile tears welled up in Tom's eyes. All he'd wanted to do was something good, but he'd made a terrible mess. He was sure a scolding was coming, maybe even a spanking. But his father just watched him. Then, walking through the mess, he picked up His crying son, hugged him and loved him, getting his own pajamas white and sticky in the process. That's how God deals with us.

We try to do something good in life, but it turns into a mess. Sometimes we just stand there in tears because we can't think of anything else to do. That's when God picks us up, loves us, and forgives us, even though some of our mess gets all over Him. Admit your inadequacies, and invite the Lord to clean up the mess you have created. Your boss, parents, friends, spouse…may say this is it, it's over! But the Lord is ever willing to take you back when you genuinely come to Him in repentance. Let Him clean up your mess.

BUILDING YOUR HOUSE

The scriptures is succinctly clear that we should pay more attention to laying up treasures in Heaven Mathew 6:19-20 puts it this way, "Lay not up for yourselves treasures upon earth, where moth and rust doth corrupt, and where thieves break through and steal: But lay up for yourselves treasures in heaven, where neither moth nor rust doth corrupt, and where thieves do not break through nor steal."Amassing wealth here on earth without corresponding riches in heaven is a complete waste. Take time to build up yourself in the 'most holy faith.' Invest in the things of the Spirit. Be spent and be willing to spend for the sake of the gospel and you would be surprise how great a treasure you have laid up for yourself.

I read a story of an elderly carpenter who was ready to retire. He told his employer-contractor of his plans to leave the house-building business to live a more leisurely life with his wife and enjoy his extended family. He would miss the paycheck each week, but he wanted to retire.

The contractor was sorry to see his good worker go and asked if he could build just one more house as a personal favor. The carpenter said 'yes,' but over time it was easy to see that his heart was not in his work. He resorted to shoddy workmanship and used inferior materials. It was an unfortunate way to end a dedicated career.

When the carpenter finished his work, his employer came to inspect the house. Then he handed the front-door key to the carpenter and said, "This is your house... my gift to you."

The carpenter was shocked!

What a shame! If he had only known he was building his own house, he would have done it all so differently.

Don't wait until it's late. Commit your time and energy to serving the Lord now because those that diligently seek and serve Him will never lose their reward. Give of your best to the Master and give Him the strength of your youth. I pray that after all the labor and toiling, may we never lose our reward at the end of the day.

CHAPTER FOUR

CONTENDING FOR THE FAITH

THE LETHAL BLEND

During the era of the apostles, they were identified as Christians because they lived the Christ-like life. They didn't scream that they were Christians just to be recognized as such; their life reflected righteousness. They were the salt that quietly went about enriching and preserving the lives of others. However, the church today is likened to the 'salt that has lost its savor.'

A young police officer was taking his final exam for the police academy, and he read the following question in the exam paper: You are on patrol in the

A WALK INTO ETERNITY

outer city when an explosion occurs in a gas main on a nearby street. Upon investigating, you find that a large hole has been blown in the footpath and there is an overturned van nearby. Inside the van, there is a strong smell of alcohol. Both occupants—a man and a woman—are injured. You recognize the woman as the wife of your Chief of Police, who is presently out of town. A passing motorist stops to offer you assistance, and you realize that he is a man who is wanted for armed robbery. Suddenly, a man runs out of a nearby house, shouting that his wife is expecting a baby, and that the shock of the explosion has made the birth imminent. Another man is crying for help, having been blown in the adjacent canal by the explosion, and he cannot swim. Describe in a few words what actions you would take. The young man thought for a moment, picked up his pen, and wrote, "I would take off my uniform and mingle with the crowd."

A WALK INTO ETERNITY

Some of us see the Christian life in the same way. We see the Christian life as trying to juggle five or six balls at one time whilst balancing a jug of water on our heads. And when the pressure gets too much, we want to give up and mingle with the crowd. We spend our time trying to pass what we perceive to be "God's exam" so that we will be "holy." There is a perception about the church today that we have lost our 'salt'. In Bible times, salt was very important. It was used to preserve and enrich things. We introduce ourselves as Christians, and people look around thinking you are talking about someone else. Churches are found on every street with loudspeakers blaring into the air. In some cases, three to four churches share a building, and yet evil and wickedness is being perpetrated by the same people who throng, and sometimes lead, these places of worship. Some, as result of their deep pockets, have even gone ahead to become church leaders, cabals, and power brokers, and the pastor dares not to speak against their wantonness and evil because he fears they will get angry and leave the church to the ever waiting hands of another pastor who will gladly welcome them and their contributions. These pastors think, '*Oh! What an answer to my prayers. At least the tithe portfolio will now increase, and I can enjoy the same luxury of Pastor X, Y, and Z.*' This is quite disturbing! You have blood on your hands already. No wonder the light has gone out! We make so much noise but no impact. It wasn't so from the beginning. Rascals in suits have taken over the pulpit and with their oratory have swept many away from the core spiritual principles that have been the bedrock of our faith. We have blended in. The world is in the church and the church in the world…you cannot spot the difference anymore. People now equate success in ministry to the number of churches established and the corresponding mammoth follower-ship they enjoy, and yet no difference is seen, even on the streets where these churches are located. This allows evil to thrive continually.

A WALK INTO ETERNITY

The church has failed to tell the people that, even though our God is love, He is equally a consuming fire. Building church membership is the principal focus this. Don't get me wrong, there is nothing wrong with this, but we should make sure that we are teaching our members,-old and new- the truth about God and His word. We should not censor our messages because we don't want them to leave our churches and take their money elsewhere. We affirm the need for the money as we work to build our big cathedrals and compete with one another in the process. We have lost focus. We are running blind of our final destination. Enough of the 'big man' gospel that impoverishes the soul! Let's share the truth of the Word and earnestly contend for the faith that was once delivered unto the saints. The pulpit use to be a place of penitence, holiness, prayer, and the Presence of God, but today you see that glitz, glamour, and razzmatazz have taken the place of these priceless virtues. It's little wonder why people who see such things go ahead to learn the pulpit theatrics so they can fit in and sway the ever gullible public. We need to get back on track. Be the light that God has called us to be. Heaven is searching for men who will not sell their soul in exchange for a morsel of bread! What will count at the end is what the Lord will say of you when you come face to face with Him. Think about it!

GOD'S UNWAVERING STANDARDS

God cannot lower His standards. That others (no matter how great they are in ministry) have lowered their standards to accommodate the changing times in the world does not mean God has lowered His. The story is told of a man who rushed into a suburban railroad station one morning and, almost breathlessly, asked the ticket agent: "When does the 8:01 train leave?"

"At 8:01," was the answer.

A WALK INTO ETERNITY

"Well," the man replied, "my watch says it's 7:59, the town clock says it's 7:57, but the station clock says it's 8:04. Which clock am I to go by?"

"You can go by any clock you wish," said the agent, "but you cannot go by the 8:01 train. It's already left."

He had missed his train by "that much" because he didn't pay attention to the right standard.

If you are governed by the wrong standards, you will 'miss the train.' Let God's Word be your guide. It's got the 'accurate time.' I encourage you to flee from anything that will pollute your soul no matter how well garnished those things are. Let us stand for the truth. Hold on to righteousness even if you are the only one standing. It will not be a funny scene if you don't 'catch the final train.' Think about it!

A WALK INTO ETERNITY

WHY ARE YOU NOT HERE?

How many of us have sold out? We have betrayed the Lord because we felt help would not come, and then we decided to play 'God' by doing it our way or, better still, the popular way. This is the time for you to look inward and re-evaluate where you stand in your walk with God. Ask yourself this question and don't wait to be asked on the final day after the rapture when the same people who sang your praises and led you on will come to your doorstep and ask, 'why are you still here?' Think about it! May the Lord count us all worthy of His Kingdom.

There was a story about how Hitler imprisoned a German pastor, Martin Niemoeller, for eight years. The Pastor spent some time in prisons and concentration camps, including Dachau. Hitler realized that if Niemoeller, a First World War hero, could be persuaded to join his cause then much of the opposition would collapse. So he sent a former friend

A WALK INTO ETERNITY

of Niemoeller to visit him, a friend who now supported the Nazis. Seeing Niemoeller in his cell, the one-time friend is reported as saying, "Martin, Martin! Why are you here?" To which he received from Niemoeller the response, "My friend! Why are you not here?"

This is a question we need to reflect on. *Why are you not here?* As a Pastor, Minister, Church worker, Deacon, Leader (or whichever is applicable), you have taken the route of convenience and compromise. You have chosen the path where the crowds are always singing your praise, but won't dare tell you the truth. You have become men pleasers and abhor everything called Truth. You wallow in your wantonness and deride those who stand for Godliness and Righteousness. *You are not here* because you cringe at what your friends would say when they realize the path you have chosen. The thought of what the world would say about your stand makes you betray your conscience. *Why are you not here?* You say you want to belong; you want to flow with the present tide. A little here, a little there doesn't hurt you may think, but you have failed to realize that a drunkard doesn't get drunk with the first sip from the bottle; it takes the accumulation of several sips for him to get intoxicated. *'Here'* is a place of commitment. It is a place where we have made up our mind not to bow down to 'King Nebuchadnezzar' and with an affirmation in our heart that even if we are not delivered, we will not renounce our faith in the Lord.

WHERE IS GOD'S GLORY?

God will never share His glory with any man. God shares His love, power, grace, mercies, and all other great blessings with His people, but there is something He will never share with man and that is His glory. Unfortunately, some pastors and people in ministry have attempted to replace God with themselves, and have awarded themselves the glory that is due to God. It is a terrible thing to take the glory that is meant for the Lord. No matter how anointed you are, when you create an impression amongst your flock that the problems in their lives ends with you, then you are putting yourself in the place of God in their lives. You put the people under 'lock and key,' and you manipulate them at will. You have sermonized and taught them to be more dependent on you and less dependent on God even though you don't admit to this. God cannot compromise His glory. In the old and new testaments, people paid dearly for usurping the glory that belongs to God.

When you fail to realize that God is the source of all that you are today, then you are balancing on a thin line over a pit that leads to your doom. Your life and ministry requires balance. Remember the days when you started in ministry: how humble and how lowly in heart you were. How you would pray and seek the

A WALK INTO ETERNITY

face of God tirelessly knowing fully well that He is your backbone. When people want to help you with your bible and stand as your 'armor bearers,' you maintained your demeanor refusing to be cajoled into it (it isn't like there is anything wrong with someone helping to carry your bible). You made up your mind not to be bamboozled by the pressures of ministry and lower the standard of the Word of God. You were a truth soldier, and your motto was 'others may but I cannot.' Then the Lord began smiling on you, and your diligence and labor in ministry began to experience a turn around. Before you know it, your church grew and had to move to a bigger space. Things changed dramatically for you, and mighty works were being wrought through you. Then gradually, you get overwhelmed by the successes that have greeted the ministry. Prayer time began to drop and then vaporized completely. You scooped the inspiration and knowledge of other men to move 'stuff' on the pulpit instead of hearing directly from God. Now, you have an 'armor bearer' who takes off your coat for you, puts your shoes on your feet, stands behind you when you minister, and wipes your sweat from your brow as you stand on the pulpit. If it were possible, he would carry you to the podium if you so desired. At this point, the flesh begins to over-ride the Spirit. You begin to lose sight of God and see yourself in His place. Unfortunately, you are in denial and, just like Samson, the Spirit of God has departed from you. You think since the miracles still happens and the men pleasers are still giving their approval, then all is well. That's why I often think the pulpit is one of the most subtle routes to hell. You may be on the path to hell and never know it until it's too late. The modern day church has drifted. A lot of practices that are alien to the church have been introduced in a bid to be millennium compliant. You hear phrases like 'the world is changing and, as a result, the church must step up her game.' It has become a rat race with the church competing to become like the world and the world drifting farther and farther from the reach of the church. Now, don' t misunderstand me: there is nothing wrong with the church introducing changes that will help with accomplishing her mission, but this should not mean adapting ungodly methods all in the name of expanding our reach.

What has happened to you, Man of God? You now put a price tag on the gifts that God has graciously bestowed upon you. If an invitation to preach does not include a first class ticket, 5 Star hotel accommodation, expensive continental dishes custom prepared for you, and a categorical statement of what your honorarium should be you won't honor such invitation. You may even tell a church or organization that they can't afford you. You reject invitations that will not pay you more, and accept those that are sure of the financial outcome. You have failed to realize that God made you who you are, and He knows every motive behind your actions. That's why I believe there will be a lot of surprises on the final day.

"Let him that thinks he stands, take heed let's he fall" (1 Corinthians 10:12). Make every conscious effort to glorify God before the people. Moses suffered for this. God will not lower His standards. If He did not do the same for Moses, who was considered the meekest man on earth in his time, He will not allow you to get-away with it either. My deepest prayer has been, 'after having done all, to be found standing.' The Lord will help us all.

BURNING AND SHINNING LIGHT

> *"Words which do not give the light of Christ increase the darkness."*
> *- Mother Teresa*

There is so much pressure to change the message of the gospel, and even now a lot of people have succumbed to that temptation. Jesus is no more the core of our messages. Our messages are now focused more on how to prosper and live the good life. In as much as there is nothing wrong with teaching people this principle, let us make Jesus the foundation. The prosperity gospel has gradually taken the place of righteousness. The emphasis of our sermons every Sunday is how we can nourish our bodies and yet impoverish our souls. The people get fat and sumptuous, but at the end their soul is banished into hell because we fail to keep the 'light of Jesus and His Righteousness burning.'

There is an old story about a lighthouse keeper who worked on a rocky stretch of coastline. Once a month, he would receive a new supply of oil to keep the light burning so that ships could safely sail near the rocky coast. One night, though, a woman from a nearby village came and begged him for some oil to keep her family warm. Another time, a father asked for some to use in his lamp. Another man needed to lubricate a wheel. Since all the requests seemed legitimate, the lighthouse keeper tried to please everyone and grant the requests of all.

A WALK INTO ETERNITY

Toward the end of the month, he noticed his supply of oil was dangerously low. Soon it was gone, and one night the lighthouse went out. As a result, that evening several ships were wrecked and countless lives were lost. When the authorities investigated, the man was very apologetic. He told them he was just trying to be helpful with the oil. Their reply to his excuses, however, was simple and to the point: "You were given oil for one purpose, and one purpose only – to keep that light burning!"

This is true about many of us today. The resources may be lean but the Source is ever fresh. Presently, so many lights have gone dim or even put out completely. You need the oil to keep the light on. The Scripture says, 'We are the light of the world, and a city set on the hill cannot be hidden.' – Matthew 5:14. We are meant to be a shining and a burning light, giving direction and being the conduit through which the Lord will save the lost world. Unfortunately, in our world today, the reverse is the case. Many who

A WALK INTO ETERNITY

once bore the torch of the gospel are losing their faith, and now they need 'The Light' themselves. The 'roaring lion' is on the loose, ferociously attacking God's people all over the world. There is a scare campaign from the enemy to weaken our faith in the Lord, but our God is an ever present help in the time of need. Keep that light burning. Stay on course and keep your focus on Jesus. Psalm 34:5 says "They looked unto him, and were lightened: and their faces were not ashamed." Keep looking unto Jesus. Are you experiencing some challenges in Ministry? Keep looking unto Jesus! Have you been blackmailed and ridiculed because you have chosen the path of righteousness? You just keep your gaze on Jesus and you will not be ashamed.

The church universal is losing her relevance. The world doesn't look up to the church anymore because we are more or less like them. Gone are the days when Kings go to the Priests, and they are told the mind of God without fear or favor. Where are the

John Wesleys, the Finneys, the Jonathan Edwards, and the John Knoxs, of which the queen of Scotland remarkably said, "I fear the prayer of John Knox more than all the army of Scotland." They paid the price. We need to go back to 'Bethel' where we first met the Lord and seek His face for Restoration. May the Lord have mercy on us, and may heaven count on you to be a torch bearer for His Kingdom.

CHANGING SHADES

Some people are chameleons in character: wherever you put them, they change to that color. Their thinking and their behavior depend on their environment. Christians are called to a different lifestyle. A lifestyle is a pattern of living wherein we live out what we believe. As Christians, we were not called to blend in. As Christians, we were called to stand out.

A WALK INTO ETERNITY

A father and son were raking leaves when they noticed something darting in and out of the piles. After careful effort, they uncovered a chameleon. It was difficult to see among the brown leaves, as it had blended with them by turning brown. After catching the little creature, they put it in a jar of green grass, where it immediately turned green. When they added some red berries, the chameleon began to take on that color. We have been called unto salvation by God. We have also been called out of the world and worldly ways in order to live out our calling to a life of holiness as we serve God. Sexual impurity has become rampant in the church because we've ignored the costly work of obedience to God's standards as individuals, asking too often, "How far can I go and still be called a Christian?" Stretching the border lines, we've crafted an image for ourselves. We may even keep our physical bodies sexually pure while permitting our eyes to play freely when no one is around. However, this soon takes root in our hearts and will quickly lead to destruction. Keep yourself pure, for only the pure in heart will see God. Are you ready?

THE TRUE REFERENCE POINT

Who is your standard? When you make God your standard consistently, one day, you will become a standard to the world. Nuclear submarines consist of some of the most amazing technology on the planet. These incredible military vessels can stay underwater for ninety days, but every ninety days the submarine must resurface to maintain proper alignment with the North Star. While underwater, the submarine's navigational system is affected by the earth's magnetic forces. Because the submarines carry missiles of mass destruction, they must pay close attention to keeping the navigational equipment aligned to the true reference point of the North Star.

A WALK INTO ETERNITY

There is a lesson to be learnt here. We cannot perform at our highest level or complete our mission without maintaining proper alignment with our God. The day you become self-sufficient marks the beginning of your decline. Don't be carried away by the fact that you are winning every race.

CHAPTER FIVE

ETERNITY IS NON-NEGOTIABLE

HOLD ON TO YOUR CROWN

Let us hold fast to that which we have received lest another take away our crown. There is someone waiting at the corner to rob you of 'your crown.' Your crown could be your joy, peace, prayer-life, or your study of the Word. It could also be your home, or your 'ticket and visa' to heaven. Whatever it is, you need to hold fast with a firm grip. Don't let it go! Guard it diligently and jealously. Many have lost theirs and they have never recovered it back. It's difficult to build, yet very easy to destroy. Many have spent years and years building up their lives, families, ministries, and walks with God, but friends, it does not take the enemy five minutes to bring all these down if we allow him. The race is neither for the swift nor the mighty...care must be taken. Don't ever think you are infallible, for that's just a delusion from hell. 'Let him that thinks he stands take heed lest he fall.' Hold fast! Hold on!

You have a duty to guard your heart for out of it flow the issues of life. This is a full time job. You cannot delegate another to help guard your heart. It is something you have to do yourself. These days are evil. Look around you, and you will see that there is moral breakdown everywhere. People are throwing in the towel, giving up on God and themselves with some already developing a reprobate mind. The truth is gradually becoming a scarce commodity. It has disappeared from many pulpits across the world and those who were, once upon a time, the beacons of hope have slowly slipped into spiritual oblivion. Watch! Keep your eyes open. The narrow path is slippery. Put your feet to the ground. You are not the first that will travel this road. Learn from their examples, but never make man your standard. No matter how spiritually powerful and influential a person is, he is only a co-traveler with you. Make Jesus your standard, and you will never be wrong. Hold fast to the faith. I am talking about the faith of our fathers. It was the Living Faith.

TIMELESSNESS

Are you trifling with the things of eternity, living your life as if it will all end here on earth? Do you care about what happens to you after you have lived your life on this earth? Our God is compassionate but there is a part of Him that will be on display at the threshold of eternity, and it will not allow for any form of gate crashing. At that point, your topping the gospel music chart will not rescue you if your life is not right with Him. The countless millions of souls

A WALK INTO ETERNITY

we have preached to at our crusades will be meaningless, if we have not lived a holy life here on earth. Your greatest achievements and breaking world records in business and science will be as dung before you when you eventually realize you are doomed for all eternity. Beloved, eternity is timeless.

There was a king who had all the world could afford. The thing he loved most, however, was to laugh.

Once, while being entertained, a jester came along wishing to join in the festival of activities and to perform for the king. His opportunity came and he put the best comical show together he had ever done. The king never laughed so hard.

Once the activity was over, the king wanted to hire this clown to be his personal jester. Once hired, the king, in humor, handed him a small stick, and said, "You are the most foolish man alive. When you find someone more foolish than you, then you give them this stick," and the king laughed heartily. After many years had passed by, the king lay sick on his death

A WALK INTO ETERNITY

bed ready to go at any moment. He called for his jester, for he wanted to laugh one more time before he died. When the jester was through, he asked to speak to the king personally.

Once alone with the king, the jester asked, "King, where are you going?"

The king responded, "On a far journey."

The jester asked, "And how do you plan to get there?"

Again the king responded, "I don't know."

Then the jester pulled the stick from his back pocket and handed it to the king. The king was stunned, and asked why he had given him the stick. The jester replied, "King, today I have found a more foolish man than I. For you see, I only trifled with the things of life, but you have trifled with things of eternity!"

Take a minute and think about this. Eternity has no end. It means there will be no more time. Are you prepared to face the ONE who sits on the throne?

A WALK INTO ETERNITY

Mercy is available today! Don't wait until the time comes when you will seek it with tears and not find it. Do you know, I have asked myself sometimes, what use is it for me to criss-cross nations preaching the gospel, organizing programs that are changing the lives of people all over, and seeing miracles happen in the lives of others by calling on the Lord on their behalf only to miss heaven? I can't imagine it. Beloved, we need to wake up to righteousness. Eternity with the Lord is too precious to allow anything or anybody to come between us and heaven. I pray none of us will miss heaven. Make this your daily prayer.

DON'T IGNORE THE WARNINGS

The 1986 Chernobyl nuclear disaster in northern Ukraine should never have happened. Carelessness was identified as one of the factors responsible.

A WALK INTO ETERNITY

"There were two electrical engineers in the control room that night, and the best thing that could be said for what they were doing is they were 'playing around' with the machine. They were performing what the Soviets later described as an unauthorized experiment. They were trying to see how long a turbine would 'free wheel' when they took the power off it.

"Now, taking the power off that kind of a nuclear reactor is a difficult, dangerous thing to do, because these reactors are very unstable in their lower ranges. In order to get the reactor down to that kind of power, where they could perform the test they were interested in performing, they had to manually override six separate computer-driven alarm systems.

"One by one the computers would come up and say, 'Stop! Dangerous! Go no further!' And one by one, rather than shutting off the experiment, they shut off the alarms and kept going. You know the results: nuclear fallout that was recorded all around the world,

A WALK INTO ETERNITY

as the largest industrial accident ever to occur in the world."

This city, which formerly had 55,000 people, is now largely abandoned.

The instructions and warnings in the Scriptures are just as clear. We ignore them at our own peril, and tragically, at the peril of others. Why soil your hands and allow your heart to be polluted by the devil? You have silenced the voice of the Lord as He daily calls your attention to these 'unauthorized experiments' in which you have involved yourself. You ignore His warnings and think it doesn't matter. There is always a danger sign telling you to stop and don't go further. But because your conscience has been seared up, you turned deaf ears to these warnings. Why are you toiling with your life? "There is a way that seems right to man, but the end of it is destruction," says the preacher. Check your life today. Make a U-turn if need be, and the Lord will help you if you allow Him.

A WALK INTO ETERNITY

ARE YOU READY?

Annie Dillard reveals a sad, but poignant story about what happens when we set out unprepared. She tells of a British Arctic expedition which set sail in 1845 to chart the Northwest Passage around the Canadian Arctic to the Pacific Ocean. Neither of the two ships and none of the 138 men aboard returned.

Captain Sir John Franklin prepared as if they were embarking on a pleasure cruise rather than an arduous and grueling journey through one of the earth's most hostile environments. He packed a 1,200 volume library, a hand-organ, china place settings for officers and men, cut-glass wine goblets, and sterling silver flatware, beautifully and intricately designed. Years later, some of these place settings would be found near a clump of frozen, cannibalized bodies.

The voyage was doomed when the ships sailed into frigid waters and became trapped in ice. First, ice coated the decks, the spars, and the rigging. Then,

A WALK INTO ETERNITY

water froze around the rudders, and the ships became hopelessly locked in the now-frozen sea.

Sailors set out to search for help, but soon succumbed to the severe Arctic weather. They died from exposure to its harsh winds and sub-freezing temperatures. For some twenty years, remains of the expeditions were found all over the frozen landscape.

The crew did not prepare neither for the cold nor for the eventuality of the ships becoming ice-locked. On a voyage which was to last two to three years, they packed only their Navy-issue uniforms, and the captain carried just a 12-day supply of coal for the auxiliary steam engines. The frozen body of an officer was eventually found, miles from the vessel, wearing his uniform of fine blue cloth, edged with silk braid, a blue greatcoat, and a silk neckerchief – clothing which was noble and respectful, but wholly inadequate.

People may doubt the wisdom of such an ill-prepared journey. But as I wrap up my writings, a very

A WALK INTO ETERNITY

important question for us is, "Are we prepared to face eternity? It is a journey into timelessness; a journey of no return. Have we made ourselves ready for all that awaits us there?"

Physically and mentally, are we prepared to handle what may come? Do we regularly stay fit through daily study and prayer?

Are you ready? Some of us are walking blind of our final destination. Do we live as Christians? Are we spiritually ready for what lies ahead of us? To embark on a journey unprepared can set us up for disastrous results. But the good news is, you don't have to go through the journey unprepared. The Lord has made every provision for you and a large part of the success of your voyage will be determined by your regular and systematic preparation through grace and help from the Lord.

A WALK INTO ETERNITY

This is Important

I am glad you were able to read through to get to this page. I have no doubt you have been blessed reading through this book. I have come to realize that regardless of whatever a man has achieved all these will count as nothing if Jesus does not have a place in your life and if you do not eventually live with the Lord in eternity. God is interested in our success and happiness but the ultimate best day ahead is when we meet up with our Lord and Savior in glory. You cannot be a part of this if you have not surrendered your life unto Jesus and have repented from your sins. This is an invitation for you to make that commitment today and I can assure, you will never regret it. You can say this prayer:

"Lord Jesus, I thank you for this opportunity to come to you. I repent of my sins and accept you as my Lord and Savior. Please forgive and cleanse my sins. Count me worthy of your Kingdom. Give me the grace to serve you to the end. Thank you Jesus for saving me. Amen."

If you prayed this prayer, then I am happy for you. I will admonish you seek out a bible believing church where the word of God is thought in its entirety and feel free to reach me at the contact details on the next page if you do need further counsel and spiritual guidance. God bless you.

Contact Details:

Email: gmattoki@gmail.com
gbenga@gbengaowotoki.com

Website: http://gbengaowotoki.com

Facebook: www.facebook.com/gbenga.owotoki

Twitter: @GbengaOwotoki

Other Books By The Author

1. Don't Quit: Your Best Days Lie Ahead- There is A Price in The Prize

2. Kingdom Attitude For Contagious Christian Living

3. Mountaintop Boulevard: A Pilgrim's Journey into Bliss

www.ingramcontent.com/pod-product-compliance
Lightning Source LLC
Chambersburg PA
CBHW061336040426
42444CB00011B/2952